TRAPPED IN THE TAR PIT

written by
Jessica Stremer

illustrated by
Alexander Vidal

How Paleontologists Unearthed a City's Prehistoric Past

Beach Lane Books • New York   Amsterdam/Antwerp   London   Toronto   Sydney/Melbourne   New Delhi

Long before cars zoomed on streets and buildings rose high into the skyline...

ancient animals stomped, stalked, and scurried across the Earth.

Little did the animals know that something lay hidden
down,
  down,
    down,
      deep below their feet.

Until one day about
forty thousand years ago...

EARTH

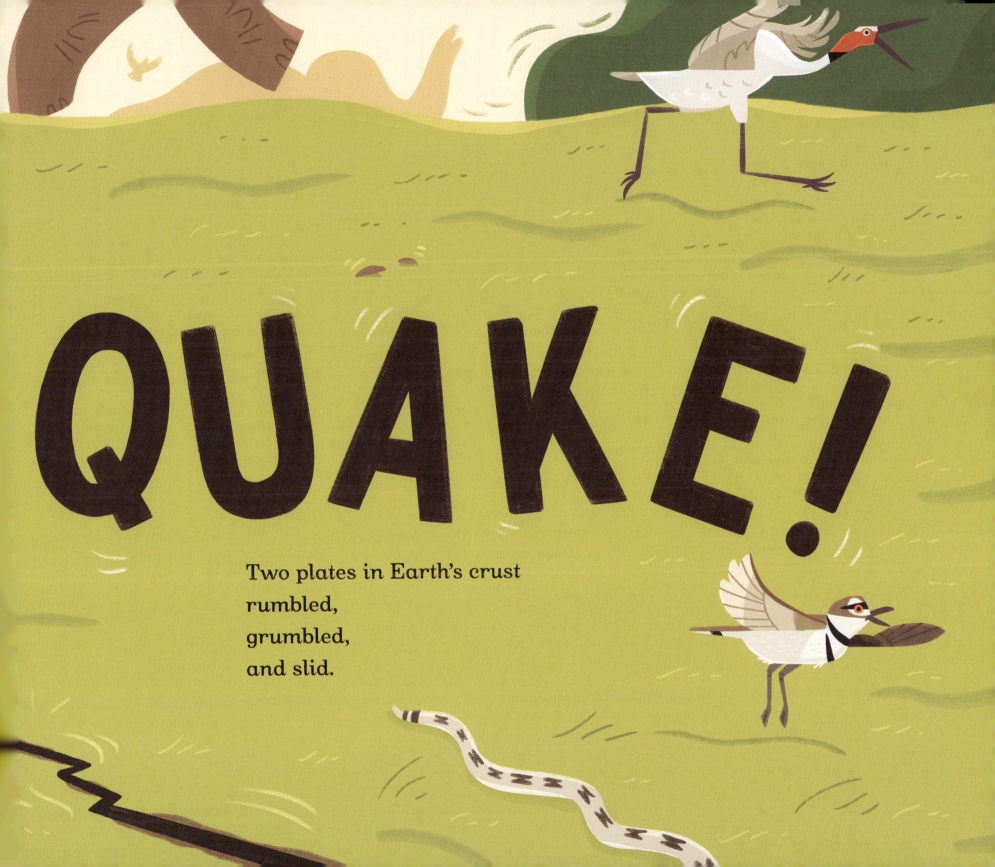

QUAKE!

Two plates in Earth's crust rumbled, grumbled, and slid.

Out of a teeny-tiny crack...

sticky tar seeped up, up, up to the surface.

But when rain fell
down,
   down,
      down . . .

it pooled on top of the tar,
hiding it once again.

An animal,
woolly and bully and thirsty from roaming,
stepped into a shallow pool for a drink.

Uh-oh! With every step, the animal's feet sank down, down, down into the tar.

The animal stretched, strained, and shifted. It tugged its feet up, up, *uuuuup.*

But no matter how hard the animal worked to get free from the sticky tar, its feet stayed STUCK!

The animal shook its head back and forth, raised its trunk high into the air, and trumpeted, Help!

Oh no . . .

The grunting and tugging and trumpeting drew the attention of hungry predators. They stalked and growled and bared their teeth . . .

The hungry animals were also trapped in the tar pit.

Stretch, strain, lift, up, pull up, *uuuugggghh!*

Thousands of years passed by.
Ground sloths, camels, and tapirs;
vultures, storks, and owls;
rattlesnakes, lizards, toads,
and many more kinds of animals became trapped.

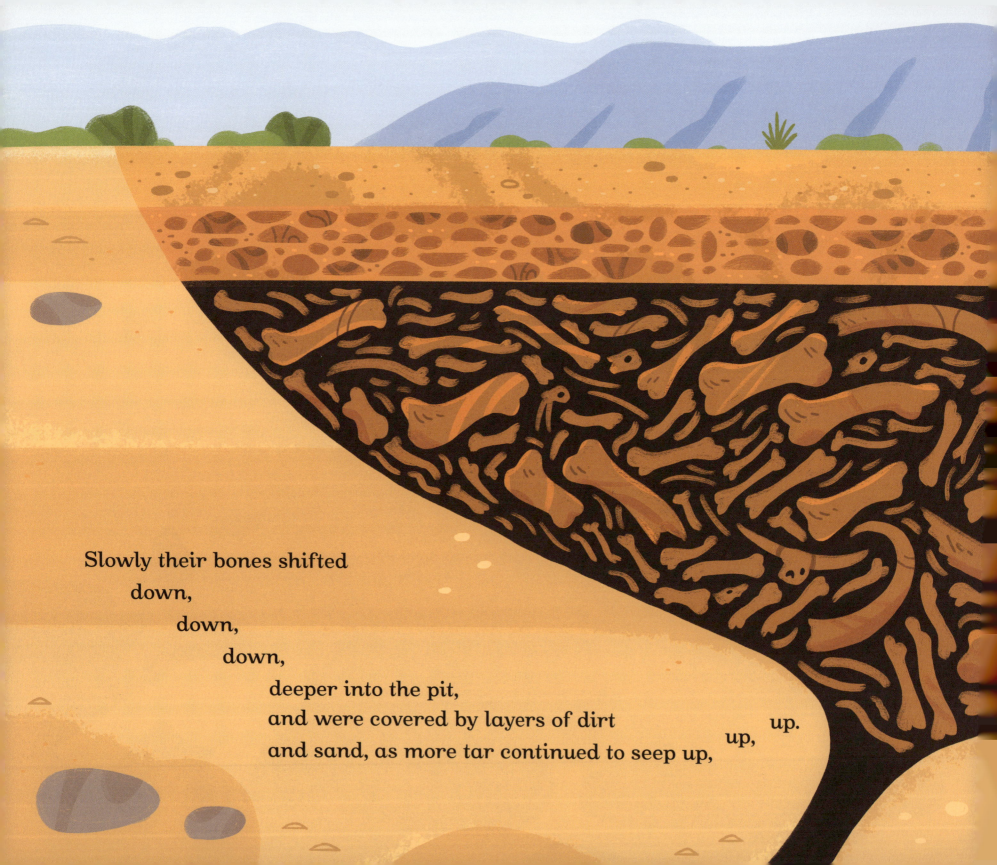

Slowly their bones shifted
down,
down,
down,
deeper into the pit,
and were covered by layers of dirt
and sand, as more tar continued to seep up, up, up.

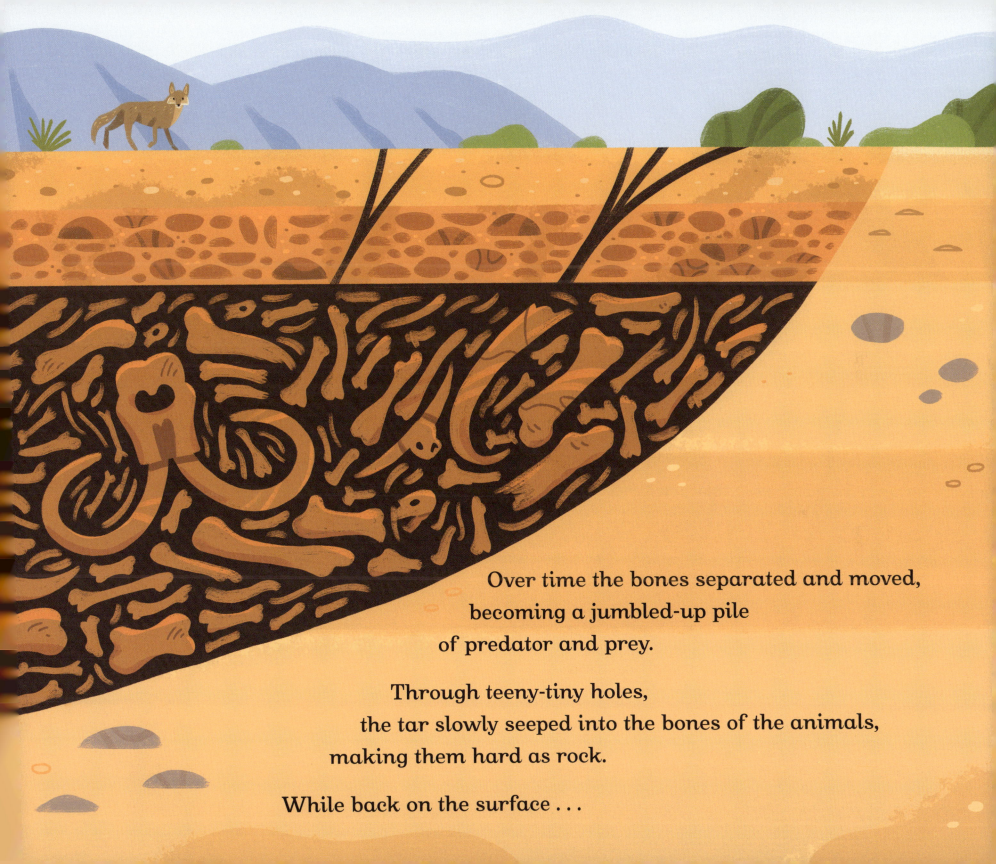

Over time the bones separated and moved,
becoming a jumbled-up pile
of predator and prey.

Through teeny-tiny holes,
the tar slowly seeped into the bones of the animals,
making them hard as rock.

While back on the surface . . .

the Earth continued to change.
At least nine thousand years ago,
humans arrived in the area.
Native Americans used the
tarlike glue to decorate clothing,
fix broken tools,
and seal baskets and canoes.

Did they know what else lay hidden
down,
down,
down
beneath their feet?

A few hundred years ago, people began mining the pit and using the tar on roofs and roads.

Every now and then,
they found bones of animals in the tar pit.
Guessing they belonged to horses and cattle,
they tossed the bones aside.

THUNK!

Until one day...

Scientists made a FEROCIOUS discovery. The bones weren't just bones. They were perfectly preserved fossils of animals that had become trapped in the tar pit thousands of years ago.

With hammers and picks they chipped, chiseled, and cleaned, then brought the fossilized bones up, up, up, back to the surface of the Earth.

But mostly people stroll, observe, and imagine an Earth where these animals ruled and roamed so very long ago.

La Brea Tar Pits Tidbits

When people think about fossils, they may imagine finding them in hard-to-reach and unpopulated places. Surprisingly, the La Brea tar pits are located in the middle of the bustling city of Los Angeles, California. But the city—and the tar pits—didn't always look the way it does today.

Over one hundred thousand years ago, parts of California were covered by water. Tar, also called asphalt, formed when the bodies of decomposed marine organisms experienced extreme pressure from water and sediment pressing down from above. Gradually the sea retreated and land-dwelling plants and animals moved in, but the tar remained trapped below the Earth's crust.

Scientists believe an earthquake around forty thousand years ago may have been responsible for creating a series of small cracks that allowed the tar to seep up to the surface. Some pools of tar were the size of small puddles, while others were as large as thirty feet across. The edge of the pit was probably only a few inches deep, increasing up to three feet deep in the center.

Cool winter temperatures turned liquid tar into a solid, which was then covered by dirt and sand that washed in from nearby streams. During summer months, tar warmed and turned back into a liquid, seeping upward once again. As more liquid tar moved to the surface, the hardened mixture of dirt and bones very gradually became buried belowground. Some areas hardened completely, while others continued to seep—even today!

Franciscan friar Juan Crespi first wrote about the tar pits in 1769, during an expedition along the coast of California. But the significance of the site wasn't realized until over one hundred years later, when Major Henry Hancock—then owner of the land and operator of the asphalt mining operation—showed an unusual bone to geologist William Denton. Denton identified the bone as a tooth from a saber-toothed cat, sparking interest and curiosity from the scientific community. Would they find other fossils in the pits?

Scientific excavations led by geologist W. W. Orcutt began in 1901. From then until 1915, the largest excavation of the tar pits occurred. Ninety-six sites in the area were excavated, resulting in over 750 thousand fossils being dug out. This included the initial excavation of Pit 91, which is still open and visible to those who visit today.

In 1969 the excavation of Pit 91 resumed. This time paleontologists documented both large and small fossils, which had previously been overlooked. Then, in 2006, new fossil deposits were discovered during the construction of an underground parking lot, including a nearly complete skeleton of a Columbian mammoth (nicknamed Zed), which is on display inside the George C. Page Museum of La Brea Discoveries.

Fantastic Finds

One thing that makes the La Brea tar pits unique is the large quantity of fossils found in a relatively small area. Scientists believe entrapment events occurring approximately once every forty years or so are the reason for this jackpot of fossil finds. An entrapment event occurred when more than one animal became trapped in a tar pit around the same time. These entrapment events most likely happened when a large, trapped herbivore attracted predators hoping for an easy meal.

Some larger animals may have been able to free themselves if the pit was small or if they didn't step too far into it. But if an animal tripped or fell, escape was probably impossible, especially for smaller animals.

Before digging begins, the excavation area is sectioned off into a grid. Paleontologists select which tools to use depending on the type of dirt surrounding the fossils. They take photographs of the area and measure the position of each fossil before removing it. A special solution is used to help remove tar attached to the fossils. The fossils are then given a protective coating. Matrix, the material removed from the ground that surrounds the larger fossils, is poured through a sifter to separate microfossils from dirt.

So many fossils have been excavated from the tar pits that scientists are still working to clean, sort, organize, and identify them! Some fossils, like pollen from plants, are so small that you need a microscope to see them. Others, like the western camel and imperial mammoth, tower over museum visitors.

Scientists use a process called radiocarbon dating as a way of telling the age of a once-living thing by measuring the amount of carbon 14 inside it. The bones of still-living animals are compared to the fossils to help identify what types of animals the bones came from.

Mammals

Dire wolves (four thousand specimens), saber-toothed cats (two thousand specimens), and coyotes (one thousand specimens) are the most common mammals discovered in the tar pits. The majority of mammals discovered are carnivores. Scientists think this is because multiple carnivores came to feed on a trapped herbivore, then became stuck themselves. Ancient bison are the most common herbivores discovered (three hundred specimens), while the imperial mammoth is the largest.

Birds

In areas outside the tar pits, fossilized birds are less commonly found than other animals because the bones of birds are hollow and more fragile. But at La Brea, fossilized birds are found in abundance. Scientists believe this is because the asphalt provided a protective coating around the bird bones, allowing them to be well preserved. The golden eagle is the most common bird (nine hundred fifty specimens), followed by an extinct species of turkey. The tallest bird discovered is the *Ciconia maltha*, a type of stork. The largest bird, a teratorn, weighed about thirty pounds and had a wingspan of about fourteen feet.

Reptiles, Amphibians, and Fish

Seven different lizard species, nine snake species, and five amphibian species have been found in the tar pits. Three species of fish have been found, all less than five inches long.

Invertebrates

Over twenty thousand specimens of mollusks (clams and snails) and well over one hundred thousand specimens of arthropods, including grasshoppers, crickets, beetles, flies, ants, and wasps, have all been found in the tar pits. Some of the insects lived in or around water and would have mistaken the pits for lakes, just like other animals did. But others, like flies, most likely became trapped in the asphalt when they came to feed on a dead animal.

Plants

Over one hundred thousand leaves, cones, seeds, and pollen specimens have been found in the tar pits. Some probably grew in the immediate area, while others may have been washed in by flood-waters or streams.

People and the Tar Pits

Only one human skeleton has ever been found in the La Brea tar pits. Scientists believe the skeleton belongs to a woman who lived about nine thousand years ago. The details of her life remain unknown. Other human artifacts include scrapers used to clean animal hides, wooden hairpins, and wooden spear tips. The most commonly found human artifacts are seashells, which were most likely obtained by trading with other tribes and used as jewelry, cups, or scoopers.

Putting It All Together

Studying fossils from the tar pits allows scientists to paint a picture of what the Earth looked like from between four to forty thousand years ago. By determining the ages of the fossils, they can tell what animals lived in the area at about the same times. Plants found in the teeth of herbivores tell scientists what those animals ate. Scientists can even study how living animals have changed by comparing them to their fossilized relatives.

Today the La Brea tar pits are a place for people to learn about animals that used to live in the area. Visitors can also see paleontologists at work excavating and cleaning fossils and piecing together parts of the past.

Several other tar pits can be found in the United States and around the world, including Trinidad and Tobago, Venezuela, Ecuador, Peru, and Azerbaijan. Each contributes in its own way to the understanding of Earth's history, but none compare to the quantity of fossils unearthed at La Brea.

Illustrator's Note

The prehistoric time period depicted in this book, at the very end of the Pleistocene Epoch, was only about forty thousand to twelve thousand years ago—incredibly recent in geological history. Modern humans were already spreading across the world, and we were only a couple thousand years away from the development of agriculture, architecture, and the first cities. Even so, the place that is now Los Angeles (my home) would have been unrecognizable—it was much wetter and cooler, more forested, and inhabited by mammoths, giant ground sloths, tapirs, jaguars, lions, and other ancient megafauna. For this book, I set out to capture the richness of the prehistoric ecosystem. While I loved getting to illustrate so many Pleistocene creatures, it was also important to me that I include species that were alive at the time of the mammoths yet still live here today, like ground squirrels, western pond turtles, California quail, and scrub jays. Indeed, realizing that as Columbian mammoths made their seasonal migration through this area they would have been greeted by the same noisy squawking of the scrub jays that I hear on a hike today, helped me feel connected to this incredible lost age.

Species List

The animals illustrated in this book (aside from the modern horses, chickens, and the fox squirrel toward the end of the book) are all species whose fossilized remains have been found in the La Brea tar pits.

1. American lion
2. American mastodon
3. American Neophrontops vulture
4. Ancestral California condor
5. Brown-headed cowbird
6. California quail
7. California ground squirrel
8. California scrub jay
9. California tapir
10. California turkey
11. Columbian mammoth
12. Coyote
13. Dire wolf
14. Dwarf pronghorn
15. Dragonfly
16. Flat-headed peccary
17. Giant jaguar
18. Great egret
19. Gopher snake
20. Harlan's ground sloth
21. Jefferson's ground sloth
22. Killdeer

23. La Brea condor
24. La Brea owl
25. La Brea stork
26. Large-headed llama
27. Long-horned bison
28. Northern flicker
29. Page's crane
30. Pleistocene black vulture
31. Pileated woodpecker
32. Red deer
33. Roseate spoonbill
34. Saber-toothed cat
35. Scimitar-toothed cat
36. Shasta ground sloth
37. Short-faced bear
38. Snow goose
39. Teratorn
40. Western camel
41. Western horse
42. Western pond turtle

To Kelly,
whose friendship I'll always cherish
—J. S.

To the climate scientists and activists
of the next generation
—A. V.

Selected Sources

Barth, Amy. "Trapped in Tar." *Scholastic SuperScience*, May/June 2017. https://art.scholastic.com/content/classroom_magazines/superscience/issues/2016-17/050117/trapped-in-tar.html?language=english#930L.

Harris, John M. *Rancho La Brea: Treasures of the Tar Pits.* Natural History Museum of Los Angeles County, 1985.

La Brea Tar Pits and Museum. "La Brea Tar Pits History." Accessed November 30, 2022. https://tarpits.org/la-brea-tar-pits-history.

National Park Service: White Sands National Park, New Mexico. "Saber-Toothed Cats." Accessed November 30, 2022. https://www.nps.gov/whsa/learn/nature/saber-toothed-cats.htm

Natural History Museum of Los Angeles County. "Saber-toothed Cat 101." Accessed November 30, 2022. https://nhm.org/stories/saber-toothed-cat-101.

Segal, Dayva. "Meet the Holy Grail of Ice Age Fossils: The La Brea Tar Pits." *AZ Animals*, July 12, 2022. https://a-z-animals.com/blog/meet-the-holy-grail-of-dinosaur-fossils-the-la-brea-tar-pits/.

BEACH LANE BOOKS • An imprint of Simon & Schuster Children's Publishing Division • 1230 Avenue of the Americas, New York, New York 10020 • For more than 100 years, Simon & Schuster has championed authors and the stories they create. By respecting the copyright of an author's intellectual property, you enable Simon & Schuster and the author to continue publishing exceptional books for years to come. We thank you for supporting the author's copyright by purchasing an authorized edition of this book. • No amount of this book may be reproduced or stored in any format, nor may it be uploaded to any website, database, language-learning model, or other repository, retrieval, or artificial intelligence system without express permission. All rights reserved. Inquiries may be directed to Simon & Schuster, 1230 Avenue of the Americas, New York, NY 10020 or permissions@simonandschuster.com. • Text © 2025 by Jessica Stremer • Illustration © 2025 by Alexander Vidal • Book design by Lauren Rille • All rights reserved, including the right of reproduction in whole or in part in any form. • BEACH LANE BOOKS and colophon are trademarks of Simon & Schuster, LLC. • For information about special discounts for bulk purchases, please contact Simon & Schuster Special Sales at 1-866-506-1949 or business@simonandschuster.com. • Simon & Schuster strongly believes in freedom of expression and stands against censorship in all its forms. For more information, visit BooksBelong.com. • The Simon & Schuster Speakers Bureau can bring authors to your live event. For more information or to book an event, contact the Simon & Schuster Speakers Bureau at 1-866-248-3049 or visit our website at www.simonspeakers.com. • The text for this book was set in Oxtail. • The illustrations for this book were rendered digitally. • Manufactured in China • 0425 SCP • First Edition • 2 4 6 8 10 9 7 5 3 1 • Library of Congress Cataloging-in-Publication Data • Names: Stremer, Jessica, author. | Vidal, Alexander, illustrator. • Title: Trapped in the tar pit / Jessica Stremer ; illustrated by Alexander Vidal. • Description: First edition. | New York : Beach Lane Books, 2025. | Audience: Ages 4–8. | Audience: Grades 2–3. | Summary: "A nonfiction picture book about one of the most exciting fossil discoveries of the modern day: tar pits!"—Provided by publisher. • Identifiers: LCCN 2024045302 (print) | LCCN 2024045303 (ebook) | ISBN 9781665953177 (hardcover) | ISBN 9781665953184 (ebook) • Subjects: LCSH: Fossils—California—La Brea Pits—Juvenile literature. | Fossilization—Juvenile literature. | Paleontology—Pleistocene—Juvenile literature. | La Brea Pits (Calif.)—Juvenile literature. | LCGFT: Picture books. • Classification: LCC QE741.2 .S77 2025 (print) | LCC QE741.2 (ebook) | DDC 560/.178—dc23/eng/20241107 • LC record available at https://lccn.loc.gov/2024045302 • LC ebook record available at https://lccn.loc.gov/2024045303